"I have known Alan for years, and his commitment to our youth has always been unwavering. Financial literacy is a foundational skill that is necessary for our young people to succeed in our economy. *Journeys with Max* is a great way to introduce those important concepts to our children."

—Texas Senator Jane Nelson

"After having the opportunity to read *Journeys with Max: Life Skills for Young People Understanding Money* by Alan Powdermaker, I had two immediate thoughts: This book should be on the shelf and curriculum of every K–5 classroom in the US, and every parent needs to have a copy at home and start reading it to their children and practicing its message at a very early age. Along with delivering essential knowledge about money, Powdermaker helps children and their parents apply that knowledge into real learning that will positively affect present and future financial decisions. A definite must-read!"

—Rodger Bennett, retired Vice President of Instruction and Executive Dean of Brookhaven College in Dallas, Texas.

"An active learning experience about money life skills focusing on family/community support. This entertaining book provides the basic habits young people need to learn to build a foundation for their future spending, saving, and giving habits. Looking forward to seeing what other money life skills Max and his family learn from future series of this book."

—Dr. Beverly Kraska, PhD, Education

"This book is GREAT! And I mean it to the extreme. I just hope that the marketing plan is a great one so that every child gets the chance to listen to/read this book. And all parents. I see it as a great gift for every occasion."

—Lois Higgins, *Entrepreneur*

Journeys with Max is an enjoyable read and easy for families to follow. Education isn't just in our schools; it begins at home at a very young age. From the business perspective, we need to work with our youth about financial literacy at the youngest ages. We need to start entrepreneurship early in life-not when they get out of college! *Journeys with Max* allows parents to have a tool to easily work with, and it gives children space to create financially and to dream. We are thrilled to have this book available in our community and that Alan has taken his passion for youth financial literacy and made it understandable and functional."

—Mary Jo Coulehan, Executive Director Pagosa Springs Area Chamber of Commerce

"*Journeys with Max* is a charming and informative financial literacy guide for young people that is highly recommended for school, public libraries, and the general public.

—Betty Church, public reference and university librarian (retired)

Journeys With Max

Journeys With Max

Life Skills for Young People
Understanding Money

ALAN POWDERMAKER

ILLUSTRATIONS BY TASHIE NEVAREZ

Clovercroft Publishing

Journeys with Max

©2020 by Alan Powdermaker

Published by Clovercroft Publishing, Franklin, Tennessee

Edited by Adept Content Solutions

Cover Design by Jill Powdermaker

Interior Design by Adept Content Solutions

Printed in the United States of America

ISBN 978-1-950892-66-2

Dedication

How do I properly say "thank you" to the one person who not only guided my early life with great love and care, but gave me a very real sense of who I was and who I could become. Morris Powdermaker was my dad and the person who I credit with providing me lessons about life as well as cautions about forks in the road. An independent businessman and professor of business economics at University of Baltimore, he taught lessons that were usually conducted at the family dinner table and always challenging but definitely a learning experience. His questions were direct, tough, and thought provoking. My answers were designed to give me perspective. It worked!

I don't remember Dad ever owning a credit card, but I do remember his admonishment about the difference between "need" and "want." He also made the point that if I can't pay for it, I don't need it. There were a lot of lessons learned at that table, and I grew a bit from each one.

Borrowing money and living on credit would never become options in my life. Almost everything I did, every decision I made, was designed to prove to him that I had learned my lessons well. Journeys with Max and the advancement of financial literacy education for young people has become a passion for me. Wherever God has taken him, Dad is quietly smiling, and I know I have made him proud once more. Saying thank you just doesn't seem to be enough, but he knows.

Foreword

This series of books is dedicated to the millions of young people who will hopefully never fall into a financial trap of their own making. We know that given the proper instruction and tools at an age as early as kindergarten, our sons and daughters and grandchildren will be able to travel through life with relative financial ease and, most certainly, success. There is no reason to amass thousands of dollars in tuition and credit card debt or forge ahead without secure bank balances or planning considerations that will lead to a well-deserved retirement.

We *implore* all of you parents, grandparents, and teachers who do not talk about money to the young people of today to jump aboard the bandwagon. We are also reaching out to corporations, banks, community organizations, and churches to help carry the banner. You can make a difference, and you know it.

Life Skills for Young People: Money will help provide some of the tools that are needed by our young people today, more than ever. Even if you were never, ever given the opportunity growing up to benefit from these lessons, you can still gain knowledge and skills that will certainly be useful as you provide financial instructional leadership. We hope that you will reach out to your schools, teachers, and administrators and encourage them to promote requirements that every child must complete certain financial literacy courses before they can graduate from high school. Let's not deny another generation the opportunity to learn positive lessons about *money*, which are meant for their benefit.

It is a privilege to be able to share this first of three volumes featuring the Journeys of Max as he matures and becomes ready to face the world. So please join us on this journey as we wish that you also acquire knowledge as well as enjoyment and the joy of teaching.

Thank You
Alan

P.S. Please use the "Resource" section of this book to find almost every type of instructional opportunity that is needed in your own travels.

Max   Sasha   Mom   Dad
           (sister)

Introduction

Comments from a 55 year old mother of two:

"I cannot see a future. I am convinced I will die before I resolve these school loans and financial issues. I cannot sleep at night. My stomach is in knots."

- *School debt now exceeds* **1.6 trillion dollars.**

- Sixty-five percent of Americans have no money saved—even for emergencies, much less for retirement. **The 2020 pandemic highlights our national problem.**

- **Three million** Americans over sixty-five are still paying off school debt.

- Parents talk more easily about **sex** to their kids than about **money.**

- Most kids will **never** receive high-quality financial education.

- **Eighty-three percent** of American students believe that financial literacy should be mandatory in secondary schools.

- American schools are producing **substandard students** in terms of being prepared for life's challenges, including financial literacy.

- Only **41 percent** of adults have budgets.

- Sixty-nine percent of parents give their kids allowances averaging $9.59 per week, but most allowances are not tied to performance of regular chores.

- Kids save about **42 percent** of their allowance while adults savings are only 8 percent of income.

- **Seven million Americans** are at least three months behind in credit card payments, averaging in excess of $10,000.

- **One half** of all Americans live paycheck to paycheck.

- **Thirty-nine percent** of American wealth is controlled by top 1 percent of the population.

- Consumer debt in America is over **four trillion dollars**.

- America ranks **seventh of fifteen** countries in financial literacy—behind China and Australia.

- **Only 24 percent** of millennials eighteen to thirty-four could answer four out of five financial literacy questions.

- Only **seven states** require at least one-half semester in financial literacy for graduation. Seventeen states have nonmandatory curriculum requirements.

But there is hope: fixing the literacy crisis starts with teaching, not with laws.

Journeys With Max

"Wow, that ball and shirt are really neat. I really **want** that ball and shirt. I think I had better talk with Dad about this."

"Dad, I saw an awesome football and a SHARK's jersey at Stars Store. The ball was only $20.00, and the shirt is one half off. I would love to have both the ball and the shirt."

"What's wrong with the football you already have?"

"It's kind of old, and the shirt is a limited edition."

"I think you and I should go in the house and talk about it."

"Max, you know that your mother and I try to buy you and your sister everything you "**need**," but you are going to have to come up with a plan to buy the things you "**want**" on your own. Understanding the difference between "wanting" and "needing" something is a really important lesson for you to learn. It will make a big difference as you get older."

 "I think you mean that you guys buy us food and clothes and other important things because we need them! Things like a new football is something I **want** and maybe could get along without. So I would have to find a way to buy those things myself. But, how do I do that?"

 "I think we need to make a visit to your piggy bank."

"Okay, Max, how much money do you have?"

 "It looks like I have only $5.25 saved up so far, and I would need at least another $15.00 just to buy the football and even more for the shirt. Maybe I could **borrow** some money from you and Mom?"

"Max, you know, if you borrow money from other people, you will have to pay it back, and many times you have to pay a fee, which is called **interest**. Finding a way to earn that money may be a smarter plan then **owing** people money."

"You mean like cutting the grass and things like that? I bet I could make a list of work things to do around the house. Do you think I could earn some extra money?"

"Absolutely, Max—we can make up a list, and if you **budget** your money well, you may be able to buy that football all by yourself."

"What's a **budget,** Dad?" (Max is scratching his head.)

"A budget is really important, Max. It is a way of guessing how much money you can earn, say, in the next six months. It also guesses what kind of needs and other expenses you will have. The difference between what you will **earn** and what your will **spend** will tell you how much money you will have left over. You can maybe spend some of that or maybe even **save** it. Your mom and I have a budget that helps us spend our money wisely and plan for the future. It kinda keeps you from having bad surprises."

"Dad, I am going to make a work list and show it to you and Mom."

"Mom, I've been doing a lot of hard work making a list of for you and Dad to see if I can earn some money for things that I **need** and maybe, **want**. This list is a lot of stuff I can do around the house." (Max is holding up chores list—clearing the table, making his bed, etc.)

 "Max that is a great list, and I am really proud of you for the work you did. But remember, Max, that some chores like helping with the dishes and making your bed are your responsibility as part of our family. We all do our share around the house so that one person doesn't have to do all the work, but we all benefit."

 "Maybe we can come up with a weekly allowance for all of those chores, including taking out the trash. You can include that money in your budget. But remember, Max, you only get your allowance if you do your chores."

"Max, let's go back and write a new list with the jobs other than your chores that you can do to make extra money, and then we can finish your budget."

 "I think I understand. My allowance will be for the chores I am expected to do around the house, and the other money I earn will come from extra jobs that need doing."

 "Great. I think you really understand. Go get that list finished, and don't forget to add raking up all of those leaves on our lawn."

"I think my lists are pretty well finished. All of that is sure a lot of work, but if I keep up with my chores and jobs, I should be able to buy that football and shirt pretty soon. But how do I plan for the rest of my money needs, and where will I keep my money?"

"Max, that is where your **budget** will come into the picture. Remember, you can only spend money that you have. The first part will estimate how much money you think you will make over the next six months and where it comes from. The next part will have three lists: **save**, **spend**, *and* **share**. That becomes your plan to see if you are making enough money for all of your needs. You may have to make a few adjustments and changes along the way. We all do."

"You mean I *can't* just spend what I can make?" (His feelings are hurt.)

"You know, Max, you will have to think about the things you will want to **save** for, like things you will want and need, even in the future. Maybe something special for school, a new game boy, or a special computer program or somebody's birthday present. Then when you get older, you will surely want a car and college will have a lot of costs. You can't start planning for all of that too soon. The money you save should go in a bank where it will be safe, and can earn you **interest**."

19

"What is this about **interest**? Dad mentioned it before—something about when you pay when you have to borrow money."

"Like I told you, when you borrow money, sometimes you have to pay **interest**, but when you put money in a bank, it earns **interest** for you. Then the bank can lend your money to people who need it and charge them interest, That's how they can pay you back. So the bank is a lot safer than your piggy bank plus you earn extra money for keeping it there."

"Wow, you mean the bank is going to keep my money safe and pay me extra money just for keeping it? That's cool. Will you guys help me get my own bank account?"

"You bet, Max. Let's get your chore list and job list started this week, and you can keep your money in your room until you are ready to put some of it in the bank. You should always keep a small amount in your piggy bank for things you will need."

"Dad, you said something before about **sharing**. What does that mean?"

"Max, we are a very lucky family. We work hard, save money and still have almost everything we **need**. Many people are not so lucky, and sometimes bad things like sickness and fires and floods happen that really hurt other families. We believe it is always good to think of others when they need help. So a piece of your earnings should be set aside for **sharing**. You can keep it in your bank or in a special box in your room, but you will decide when and how much needs to be spent and when."

"So, **saving** and **sharing** are important things I have to think about. Can I spend what's left over after **saving** and **sharing**?"

"Of course. That will be your business to decide what you **need** and what you **want**. Just remember, the things you **need** come *first*, and you don't have to ask permission, but you may want to talk with us about your plans once in a while. The money you know you want to **spend** you could also keep in your piggy bank. As you get older, you may want to help cut other neighbors' lawns or work at the grocery store.

Getting those jobs and doing good work will let you make more money for the things you may **need**. We will always be here to answer question and help you out when you ask for advice."

"I have been thinking. The family chores and even taking out the trash for my allowance is a really a good deal. I promise to do my best. My allowance will go into my **share** and **spend** jars, and the money I earn from working around the house will go into my bank account. Most of the work I can do after school before I do my homework, and trash is only once a week. Since this money goes into the bank, how often will I get paid?"

"How about every Sunday after dinner. You will have to keep good records about each job you do and how long each job takes. You can even deposit your earnings to the bank over the internet, but it is good to go to the bank once in a while. Plus your mom and I have been talking, and we are thinking that if you are really responsible, we will match what you put in the bank."

"That is really cool. I promise to be responsible and I've been thinking also and maybe I can get along with my old football until I **need** a new one. Now about that bank account: when can we go to the bank and set it up?"

"Just as soon as you save $25.00, we will make an appointment with Mr. Rush at the bank.

"Hey, you guys are leaving me out of all of this. I know how to save money too, and I want a bank account of my own! Mom, why can't I help vacuum the rugs and fold the laundry. Wouldn't that be a good way to earn extra money? And I promise to do family chores like making my bed and helping set the table. I could even feed Rufus every night." (Rufus is sitting next to Sasha, wagging tail.)

"You've got a deal, my love. Your dad and I will work up something just for you, and we can discuss it tomorrow. Meanwhile, you need to get to bed.

"Hi, everybody. Welcome to **your bank**, Max (Max is a bit confused). This is a very important day for all of us because when you become a depositor in this bank, you become one of the owners. So, in a way, we work for you and our job is to always take care of our owners and their money. We will always be here to help you with your money needs, and even help solve problems." (Max is beaming.)

"Mr. Rush, I brought $28.50 that I earned raking leaves and cleaning the car. This is money I **need** to **save**. I want to put it in "my" bank."

Mr. Rush is pointing at the list on the blackboard.

"That's a good start, Max. Now what kind of an account would you like to open? We have checking accounts, credit card accounts, certificate accounts and many different savings accounts. Over time you will learn much more about the many banking services that we can offer you, I think you need to open a **savings account**, for now, where you can deposit extra money into your bank account."

(Max smiling) "Right, Mr. Rush. I am starting to earn money that I will put away for important thing I will need as I grow older and my Dad says that this is the safest place and I will be able to earn **interest** on my money every month."

(Smiling) "You bet. I am very pleased that you understand what your bank can do for you. We also have a special "student saving program" that lets you deposit as much as you can, and we will double the interest you would usually get. You see, we want to keep you as one of our owners and help you grow your savings. If you ever want to withdraw or take out money, just come to the bank, and we will help you. Also, Max, we will set up a special password for you and your parents so you can go online anytime and see how much money you have in your account and what it has earned. Do you have any questions, Max?"

"No, this is a lot to learn, but I think I am beginning to understand most of it, and my mom and dad are going to match what I deposit from my jobs. I'm going to be rich someday!"

"Okay. Remember, I am always here for you if you have any questions. Now, once we sign some papers with you and your parents, how would you and Sasha like to see the giant safe where we keep all of your money?"

(With a big grin) "Wow, that would be cool!"

"So, you can see how safe your money is and all of these boxes are for our customers to put important documents and things for safekeeping. Someday you will want a safety box of your own."

Max and Sasha are amazed and very pleased.

"So, tell me, Sasha, when can we expect you to open an account with our bank?"

(With *big* smile) "Oh, I am already working on it, Mr. Rush!"

"Max, you get to keep your pen and bank notebook to keep your own records, and here is a pen and a notebook just for Sasha as well."

(At the same time) "Gee, thanks for everything, Mr. Rush."

"Max and Sasha, your mom and I are so proud and excited for you guys and your futures. You have both learned a great deal about money, and you should feel very special. It will be lots of fun for your mom and me to work with you."

Journeys with Max

Life Skills—Money Management

Let's see what you have learned from Max's experiences.

1. When you really want something, you (Insert pic of Max) have to _____ for it.

2. Knowing the difference between _____ and _____ is really important!

3. If you borrow **money**, you have to _____ it back.

4. Borrowed **money** charges an _____ fee.

5. You might earn an _____ if you do certain helpful chores around the house.

6. If you don't do what you promise you won't get _____.

7. Saving money in a bank can earn you _____.

8. Besides saving and spending money, we need to _____.

9. Working _____ and taking _____ in what you do makes you feel good.

(Answers)
work, want, need, allowance, interest, paid, pay, share, pride, hard

Life Skills—Money Management
Volume II Ages 9–13

Max continues to grow and learn. Join us on part two of his exciting journey.

Subject Matter

- Saving
- Sharing
- Spending
- Earning money
  - Jobs/ money earned
  - Family chores/allowance
- Setting goals, not just dreams:
  life skills: family, education, finance
- Budgeting for financial success
- More about banking
- Investing ABC's
- Keeping records
- What about credit cards?
- Paying bills and avoiding debt

Life Skills—Money Management
Volume III Ages 13–17

Max has learned so much about managing money, but now in high school, he is facing new challenges and decisions that will have a major influence on his future.

Subject Matter
- Reviewing your goals: needs, wants, education, and money matters
- Earning money to meet goals: getting a job while in school
- Other opportunities to make money
- Paying taxes and keeping records
- Investing for the future
- All about credit cards and credit scores: the dos and don'ts!
- Planning for purchase of special needs
- Updating your budget and planning your use of time
- Being smart about expense and creating debt

Life after high school
1. Planning for college plus
   - Field of study
   - Availability of schools
   - Costs
   - Family and Other Personal Resources
   - Scholarships and grants—local, state, federal, corporate
   - School, community and foundation—other resources

2. More opportunities
   - Special skills schools (using your talents)
   - On-the-job training—paid apprentice (interests)
   - On the job training—unpaid, internships
   - Military and other opportunities

Journeys with Max

One Last Word from the Author

Discovering Max and his family was a great joy for me since it allowed me to explore a subject that has become a passion in my life. I must admit, however, that my entire life has been made up of many causes and passions, and for that, I am grateful. I will always honor my parents for their guidance and direction. I am proud to have known and benefited from my brilliant aunts, Dr. Florence Powdermaker and Dr. Hortense Powdermaker, my early education at St. Paul's School in Baltimore and, of course, an unimaginable four years at the amazing Johns Hopkins University. An early career that began in New York City at Colgate Palmolive, later at Litton Industries and Norton Simon, Canada Dry in New York and Northern Europe gave me the courage to launch my own business in Dallas, Texas, that I am proud to say is still a highly successful company after forty-seven years and now operates under new management. My family has been my strength and my energy and the focus of love as they have joined with me to form alliances that are structured to give back to those less fortunate.

All of this success was not by accident. I learned a lot along the way from people a lot smarter than me. But because I listened to them and followed their example, every commitment, every return to others, and every value that I cherish has given me the joy of a fantastic life and the promise of more yet to come for me and my family. It is time to pass on a lot of what I have learned, and I am confident that my daughters will continue the process for years to come.

It is important to recognize some very talented people who have made my journey truly a blessing:

Jill Powdermaker, once again, brought her artistic talent to the table and pulled my feet out of the fire more than a few times. My projects over the years could never have been born without her talent, imagination, and, above all, love.

Tashie Navarez of Pagosa Springs, Colorado, and Las Cruces, New Mexico, is beginning to learn what a talented artist and illustrator she is and will become. She made Max and his family come alive and was always coming forth with new ideas of presentation.

The third person who made all of this possible was Larry Carpenter, head of Carpenter's Son Publishing and CEO of Clovercroft Publishing. Larry has the talent, the experience, and the road maps to take the uninitiated such as me by the hand and assure me that everything was going to be alright. It was!

JHU Presidents, Dr. Milton Eisenhower, taught me the art of creating partnerships, and Dr. Steven Muller was a personal inspiration beyond mere words.

We have two more editions to finish and publish that will educate Max through college and help prepare him for a very special life. If Max needs additional help finding his way after high school and beyond, I believe we will all be there writing new editions to provide him guidance that he can share with others. Thank you all, and you know who you are!

Life Skills: Young People, Money Matters, and Financial Literacy

Resource and Reference Guide
"Fixing the Financial Literacy Crisis Starts with Teachers, Not with Laws!"

Internet and Social Media

NerdWallet.com: All about **credit cards** and other useful financial information

EveryDollar.com: Budgeting and other financial planning matters

Financialeducatorscouncil.org: How to build a Financial Education Program

Practicalmoneyskills.com: Free materials–Practical Money Skills

MyMoney.gov: Government link to free resources—Financial Resources Education

ConsolidatedCredit: Free Financial Literacy Resource

Moneycrashers: Best Financial Education Website and Resources

Nea.org: Resources for teaching Financial Literacy

Scholar.google.com: What does Financial Literacy training teach us?

Aeaweb.org: Keeping it Simple—Financial Literacy—Rules of Thumb

Eric.ed.gov: Investment Clubs Teach Financial Literacy

Ocmboces.org: Financial Literacy for the 21st Century

*Journal.mufad.org.t*r: Survey of Financial Literacy Among University Students

Diva-portal.org: Addressing Financial Literacy in high schools

www.llcc.edu: Financial Literacy for Students

www.moneyexperience.com: Persona11 Finance Curriculum

Incharge.org: Personal Finance Education—Materials distributed free to children and adults

Alison.com: Free Personal Finance Courses.

Aba.com: American Bankers Assoc.—Financial Education Programs-Financial Literacy

www.moneyexperience.com: Personal Finance Curriculum/ Middle School, High School, College

Resource Guide—Other:

How to Get a Job in High School and Beyond: Bob Striegel, Carpenter's Sons

National Financial Education Council (NFEC): Financial Literacy Programs

Career & Financial Education (CAFE): Helping students gain financial literacy-workshops, etc.

United Way: Helping Families Thrive Financially

WalletHub: Free credit reports, credit scores, monitoring, credit improvement, savings

Texas Bankers Assoc: Austin, Texas 512 472 8388- Financial Literacy Summit, Foundation

Vikki Goodwin; Texas Representative: House Bill 1182— Mandatory Financial Literacy in Texas

Texas State University (CAFE): Strategies and Initiatives— Financial Educations

National Endowment for Financial Literacy: Call 367 741 6333

Vicki Robin: "Smart About Money.org"

Children's Financial Network: Neale Godrey—Steps to raise financially savvy kids

Champlain College: Courses in Financial Literacy (Five Stars)

Liz Frazier- How to Teach Kids: Certified Financial Planner

Olney Charter HS Olney, Pa: Starting an Elective Financial Literacy Program

Dave Ramsey: We need a MANDATE!!!!
    Contact: www.daveramsey.com

Junior Achievement: Course presentations on Financial Literacy and education

BBB: Young Consumer Advocate Program

Center for Student Credit Card Ed: The ABC's of Credit Card Finance

Citigroup Financial Education Program

Council for Economic Education: Financial Fitness for life

FDIC: Money Smart

Federal Reserve Bank of Dallas: Building Wealth in the Classroom

Film Ideas, Inc: Streaming Service-Financial Literacy;
    See at: www.filmideas.com

Film Ideas: Life Skills Series (12 part DVD)
    See at: https:/filmideas.com/index.php

Frost Bank: Frost Financial Youth Academy

IBAT Education Foundation: Financial Education-Clearinghouse for kids, teachers, and parents

The Lampo Group/Dave Ramsey Office: Foundations in Personal Finance

Rising Books: Financial Literacy for Teens: Student Book

Texas Guaranteed Student Loan Corp.: Financial Literacy Coordinator

Visa USA: Practical Money Skills for Life

EverFi, Inc: EverFi Financial Literacy Platform

Global Financial Literacy Excellance Center: G. Washington School of Business 202 994 7148

See Also:National Endowment for Financial Education

Specialized Books

Blue Chip Kids: David Bianchi

Meko & The Money Tree: Eulica Kimber, Tyrus Goshay

Get a Financial Life: Beth Kobliner

Let's Meet Ms Money: Rick Grant

Rich Dad, Poor Dad: Robert Kiyosaki

Make Your Kid a Money Genius: Beth Kobliner

What All Kids Should Know About Investing: Bob Pivniek

Money Ninja: Mary Nhin & Jelena Hacks

You're Gonna Need a Bigger Wallet: Nick Erskine

Money Doesn't Grow on Trees: Delatra Hudson

Financial Peace Junior: Dave Ramsey

Go Stock, Go: Bennett Zimmerman

Personal Finance for Teens: Carol Cox

3 Little Pigs: Samuel Loya

The Money Smart Family System: Steve Economides & Annette Economides

What Is Money: Etan Boritzer

Sydney's First Piggy Bank: Ithrean Blackman & Casidy Rivers

The Financial Angel: Ava Kofke

Smart Money Kids: Hannah Raybans

Mr. Pompety: A Series: Amanda Van derGulik

Saving Like a Sloth: Markus Heinrich

50 Money Making Ideas for Kids and Teens: Amanda Vander der Gulik & Melanie Negrin

Saving for the Future: Mattie Reynolds

Lily Learns About Wants and Needs: Lisa Ballard & Christine Schneider

Marvels of Money For Kids: Paul Nourigat

Orson's Lessons in Wealth: Karl Woodhouse

Great Ways to Teach Kids About Money: Diana De Jesus

Banking on Our Future: John Bryant

Notes

Notes

Notes

_____
_____
_____
_____
_____
_____
_____
_____
_____
_____
_____
_____
_____
_____
_____
_____
_____
_____
_____
_____
_____
_____
_____
_____
_____
_____

Notes